612.7

D1297836

Brown School Media Center
2831 W. Garden Lane
St. Joseph, MI 49085
616-982-4632

BODYWORKS

Brown School Media Center
2831 W. Garden Lane
St. Joseph, MI 49085
616-982-4632

skeleton and muscles

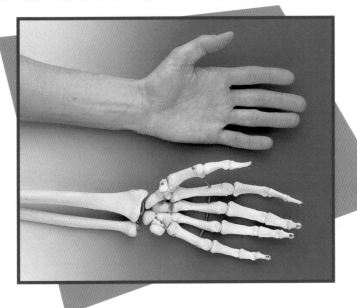

Katherine Goode

BLACKBIRCH PRESS, INC.

WOODBRIDGE, CONNECTICUT

611
GOO
FOLLETT
1-02
$17.95

Published by Blackbirch Press, Inc.
260 Amity Road
Woodbridge, CT 06525

e-mail: staff@blackbirch.com
web site: www.blackbirch.com

Text copyright ©Katherine Goode 1999

©2000 by Blackbirch Press, Inc.
First U.S. Edition

All rights reserved. No part of this book may be reproduced in any form without permission in writing from Blackbirch Press, Inc. except by a reviewer.

Printed in Hong Kong

First published 1999 by
MACMILLAN EDUCATION AUSTRALIA PTY LTD
627 Chapel Street, South Yarra 3141

10 9 8 7 6 5 4 3 2 1

Photo Credits:
Cover photo: ©Dick Smolinski
Page 1: The Photo Library/©A. & H.F. Michler; pages 18, 29: Coo-ee Picture Library; pages 24, 28: Graham Meadows; pages 13, 26, 27: Great Southern Stock; pages 12, 21: HORIZON Photos; pages 5, 15, 20: International Photo Library; page 22: Stock Photos/©Ted Horowitz; page 5: The Photo Library/©Bill Longcore; page 6: The Photo Library/©A. & H.F. Michler; page 8: The Photo Library/©Manfred Kage; page 10: The Photo Library/©Martin Dohrn; pages 7, 9, 11, 13, 17, 30: The Picture Source.

Library of Congress Cataloging-in-Publication Data

Goode, Katherine, 1949–
Skeleton / by Katherine Goode.
     p.   cm. — (Bodyworks)
    Includes index.
    Summary: Explains the various parts of the human skeleton and different types of muscles and their functions.
    ISBN 1-56711-498-9 (alk. paper)
    1. Human skeleton—Juvenile literature. [1. Skeleton. 2. Muscular system.] I. Title.
QM101.G66   2000
611'.71—dc21   00-008217
                                                                   CIP

Contents

The skeleton

Your skeleton is the bony frame inside your body. It gives your body shape.

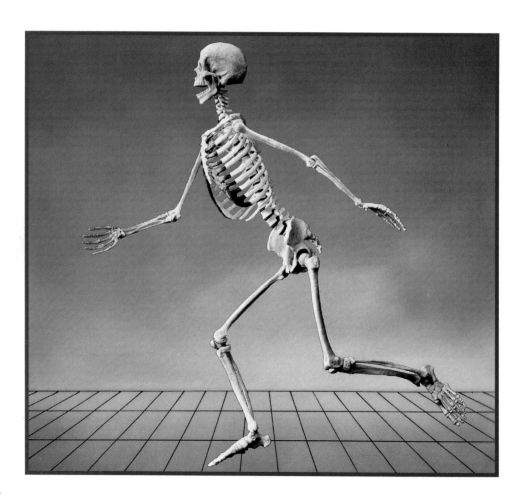

Your skeleton protects important soft organs such as your heart and brain. It also helps your body to move.

The bones

Your skeleton is made up of 206 different bones. Some bones, such as the bones in your fingers, are very small. Other bones, such as your hipbone, are quite large.

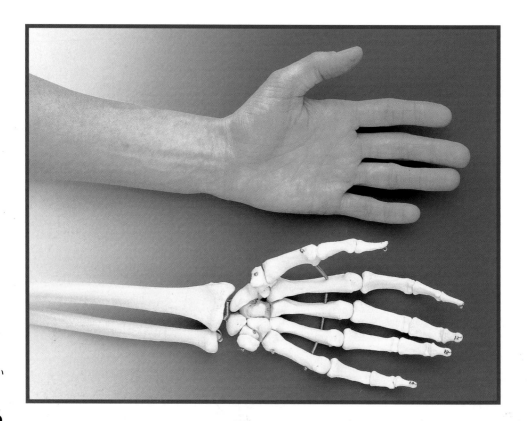

The joints

Your bones are connected by **joints**. Some joints, such as those in your skull and your rib cage, do not move. Other joints are movable. Your arms, legs, and hips have movable joints that allow you to walk, run, and jump.

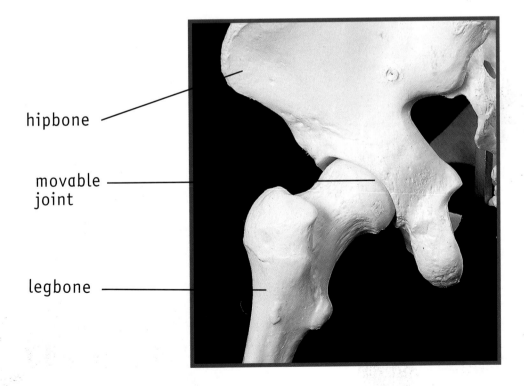

hipbone

movable joint

legbone

Parts of the skeleton

head

neck

trunk

arms

legs

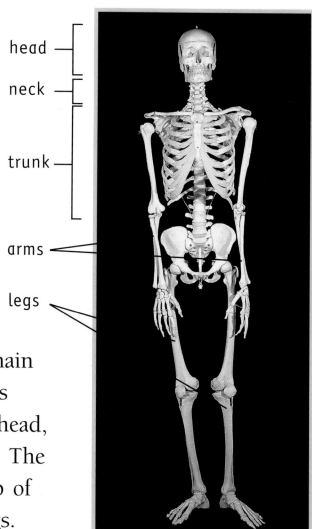

The human skeleton has 2 main parts. One part is made up of the head, neck, and **trunk**. The other is made up of the arms and legs.

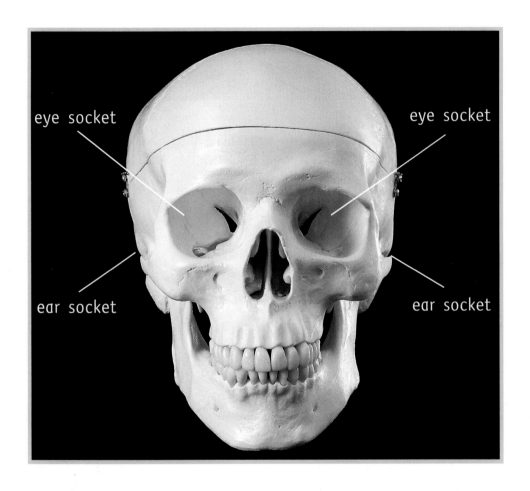

eye socket

eye socket

ear socket

ear socket

Each bone in the skeleton has a special job to do.

Your skull protects your soft brain **tissue**. It has **sockets** for your eyes and ears.

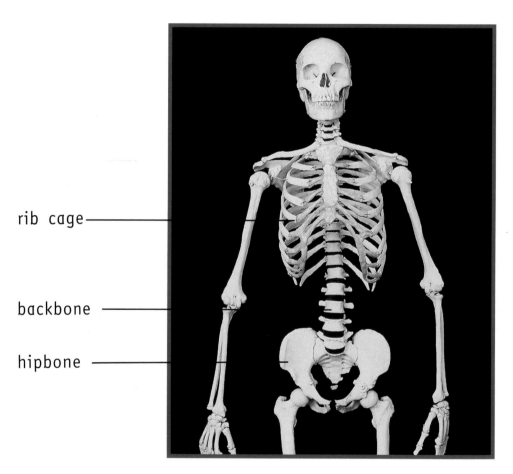

rib cage

backbone

hipbone

Your rib cage protects your heart and lungs.
Your backbone and hipbone support your whole
body. Your backbone is also called your spine or
spinal column. It is made up of separate bones
called vertebrae.

Your arm bones are used to lift and carry things. Your leg bones are used to walk and run. Your legs are attached to your hipbone, which is also called your pelvis.

Bone growth and change

The bones in babies are quite soft. Children's bones continue to grow until they become adults. By the time children become teenagers, their bones have become hard.

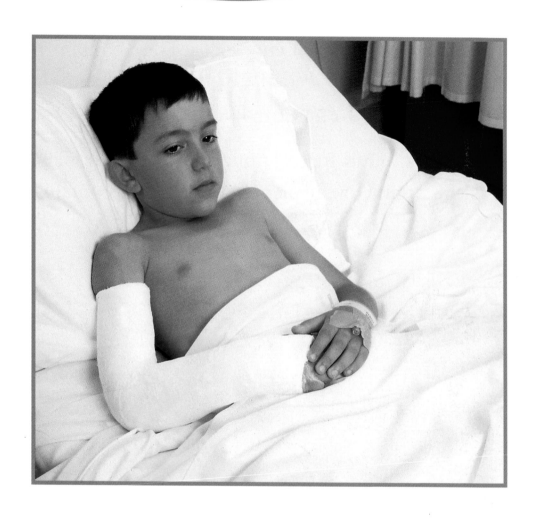

When a small child breaks a bone, it takes 3 to 4 weeks to heal. The bones in teenagers take 6 to 8 weeks to heal, because they are harder.

Bones are formed by living cells. They contain **calcium**, which is needed for growth. Calcium keeps bones strong and helps them heal.

Calcium is found in soy milk and dairy products. It is important to eat plenty of food that contains calcium to keep your bones strong.

Exercise helps to keep bones healthy.

As people grow older, their bones weaken.
Their bones lose a lot of calcium and can
become **brittle**. Broken bones in older people
often take more than 8 weeks to heal.

Animal skeletons

Birds, fish, and mammals (like you) have skeletons on the insides of their bodies.

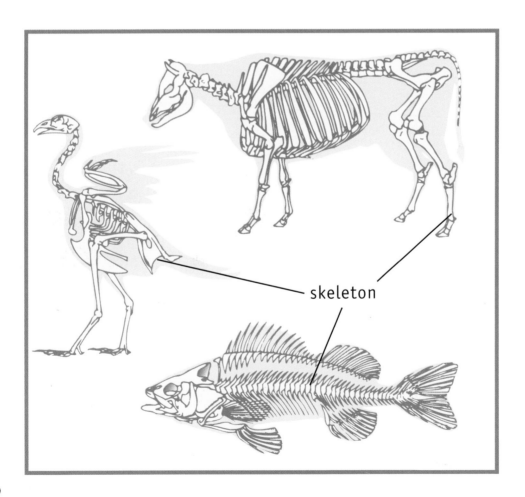

skeleton

Some animals, such as crabs and insects, do not have a skeleton inside their bodies. Instead, they have a hard outer covering. This is called an exoskeleton.

The muscles

Muscles are bundles of cells. They are attached to the bones of your skeleton and allow your body to move. The human body has more than 600 muscles!

Brown School Media Center
2831 W. Garden Lane
St. Joseph, MI 49085
616-982-4632

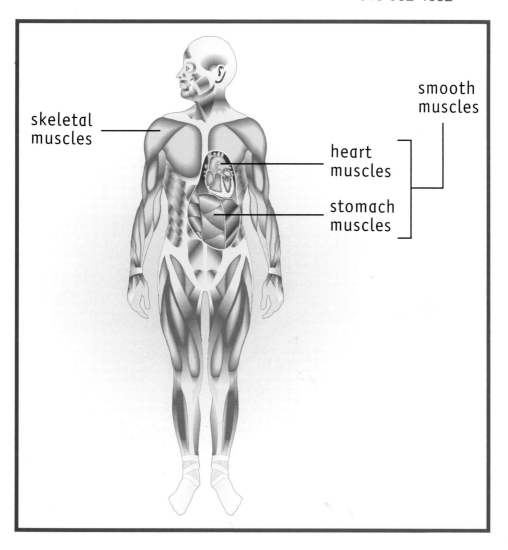

skeletal muscles

smooth muscles

heart muscles

stomach muscles

There are 2 types of muscles. Your body has skeletal muscles and smooth muscles.

Skeletal muscles

Skeletal muscles help to support the bones in your skeleton and hold your body in position. These muscles are found in your arms, legs, trunk, neck, and face.

Some skeletal muscles, such as your eye muscles, are small and weak. Other skeletal muscles, such as your leg muscles, are big and strong.

Skeletal muscles are the muscles you can choose to move. For example, when you want to close your eyes, your brain sends a message to those muscles, telling them to move.

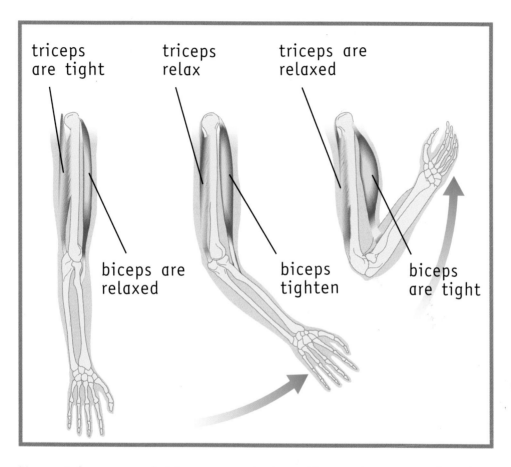

triceps
are tight

triceps
relax

triceps are
relaxed

biceps are
relaxed

biceps
tighten

biceps
are tight

Your triceps and biceps work together when you bend
your arm.

Most muscles in your body work in pairs.
When you move a part of your body, one
muscle relaxes while the other muscle tightens.

Smooth muscles

Smooth muscles are found in your stomach, heart, and other organs. These muscles move on their own. You cannot make them move.

After you eat, the muscles in your stomach help to move food through your body without you even thinking about it.

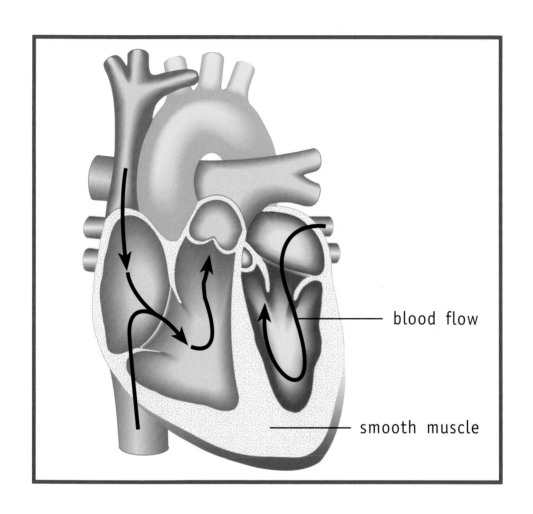

blood flow

smooth muscle

The muscles in the walls of your heart are also
a type of smooth muscle. They control your
heartbeat. Each beat pumps blood through your
body.

Muscles and energy

When you use your muscles, they give off energy in the form of heat. In cold weather, your muscles can relax and tighten very quickly. This makes you **shiver**. When you shiver, your body produces heat that warms you up.

When you exercise, your muscles give off heat.

Muscle diseases

Some people are born with muscular dystrophy, a disease that makes muscles waste away. Bell's Palsy affects the muscles in the face. Polio shrinks and weakens the muscles, but it can be prevented by a medicine called a vaccine.

Muscle growth and change

Exercise makes your muscles change shape. Muscles grow larger and stronger if a person exercises. Activities such as lifting weights, bike riding, swimming, and running strengthen muscles so they can work better.

Older people usually do less exercise than young people. Their muscles may weaken or stiffen. This makes it more difficult for them to walk. Regular exercise helps older people to strengthen their muscles and stay active.

Brown School Media Center
2881 W. Garden Lane
St. Joseph, MI 49085
616-982-4632

Eating foods that contain iron and protein helps to keep your muscles strong. Green vegetables, red meat, and dried fruits—such as raisins—contain iron. Nuts, dairy products, fish, and other meats contain protein.

Glossary

brittle	breaks easily
calcium	an element that is found in teeth and bones
joints	the place where 2 bones are connected
shiver	to shake with cold
sockets	hollows that something fits into
tissue	the matter that living things are made of
trunk	the human body, except for the head, neck, legs, and arms

Index

Brown School Media Center
2831 W. Garden Lane
St. Joseph, MI 49085
616-982-4632